4
↳19
B176m

My First Book of Sign

Pamela J. Baker

Illustrations by Patricia Bellan Gillen

KENDALL GREEN PUBLICATIONS
Gallaudet University Press
Washington, DC

Kendall Green Publications
An imprint of Gallaudet University Press
Washington, DC 20002

Library of Congress Cataloging in Publication Data

Baker, Pamela J., 1947–
    My first book of sign.

    Includes index.
    Summary: Pictures of children demonstrate the
forming in sign language of 150 basic alphabetically
arranged words, accompanied by illustrations of the
words themselves. Includes a discussion of fingerspelling and general rules for signing.
    1. Sign language—Dictionaries, Juvenile. [1. Sign
language—Dictionaries. 2. Picture dictionaries] I. Gillen,
Patricia Bellan, ill. II. Title.
HV2476.B35 1986   419   86-14937.
ISBN 0-930323-20-3

Gallaudet University is an equal opportunity employer/
educational institution. Programs and services offered by
Gallaudet University receive substantial financial support
from the U.S. Department of Education.

For Kathy Brooks
and for Katie Baker

Aa

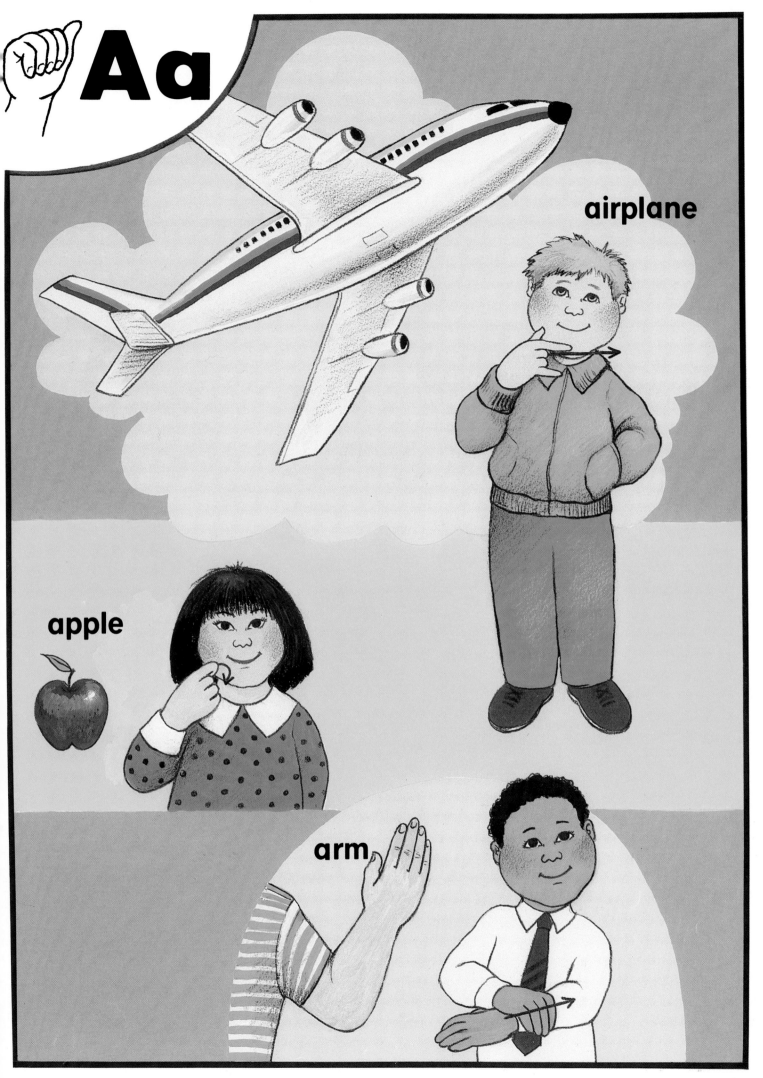

airplane

apple

arm

1

Bb

baby

ball

bear

bed

big

bird

birthday

blow

boat

book

box

boy

broken

brush

button

7

Cc

cake

candle

car

8

cat

catch

chair

climb

clock

coat

comb

come

cookie

12

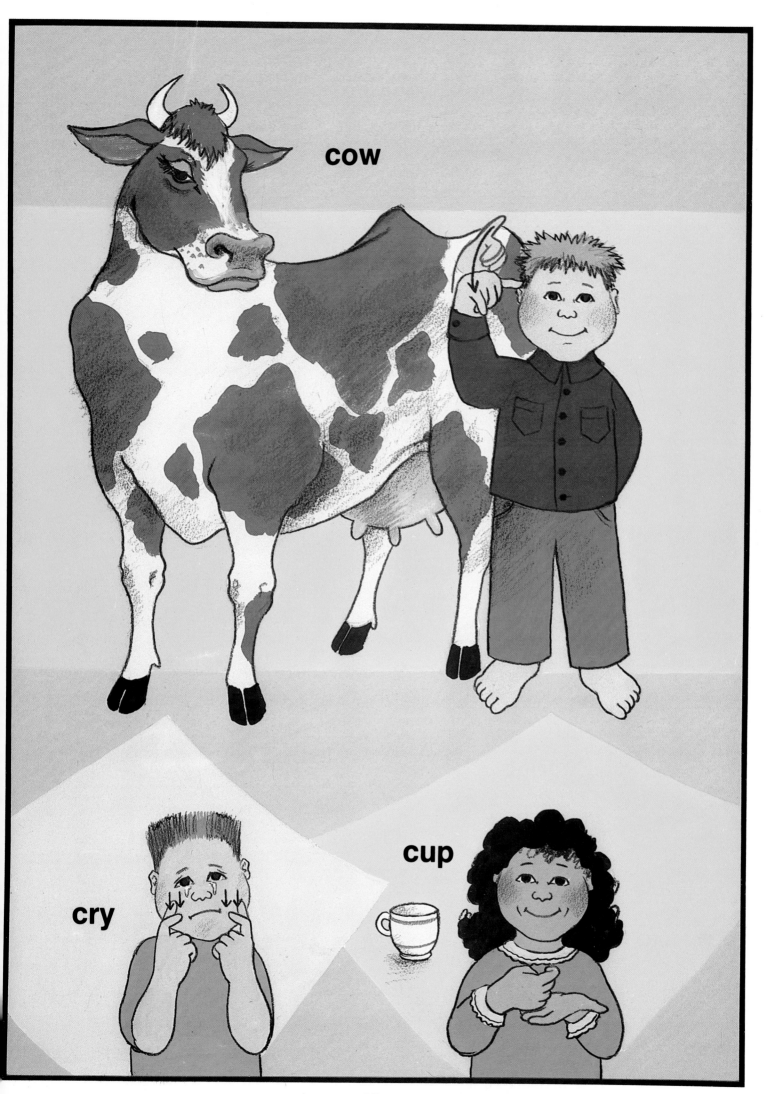

cow

cry

cup

Dd

dirty

dog

doll

door

draw

dress

drink

WATER

drive

dry

duck

Ee

ear

eat

egg

elephant

eye

Ff

face

fall

fence

finger

fire

21

fish

floor

flower

fork

frog

Gg

girl

glass

go

grow

Hh

hair

hand

happy

26

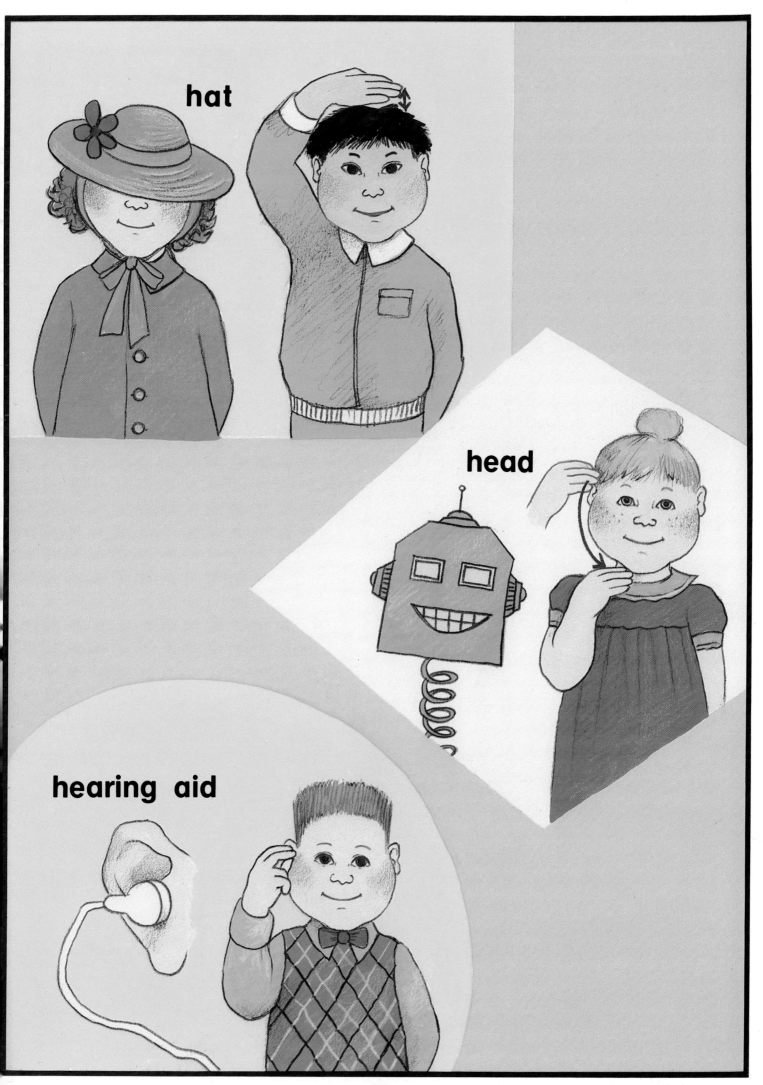

hat

head

hearing aid

hit

horse

28

hot

house

Ii

ice cream

iron

Jj

jam

juice

jump

Kk

key

kiss

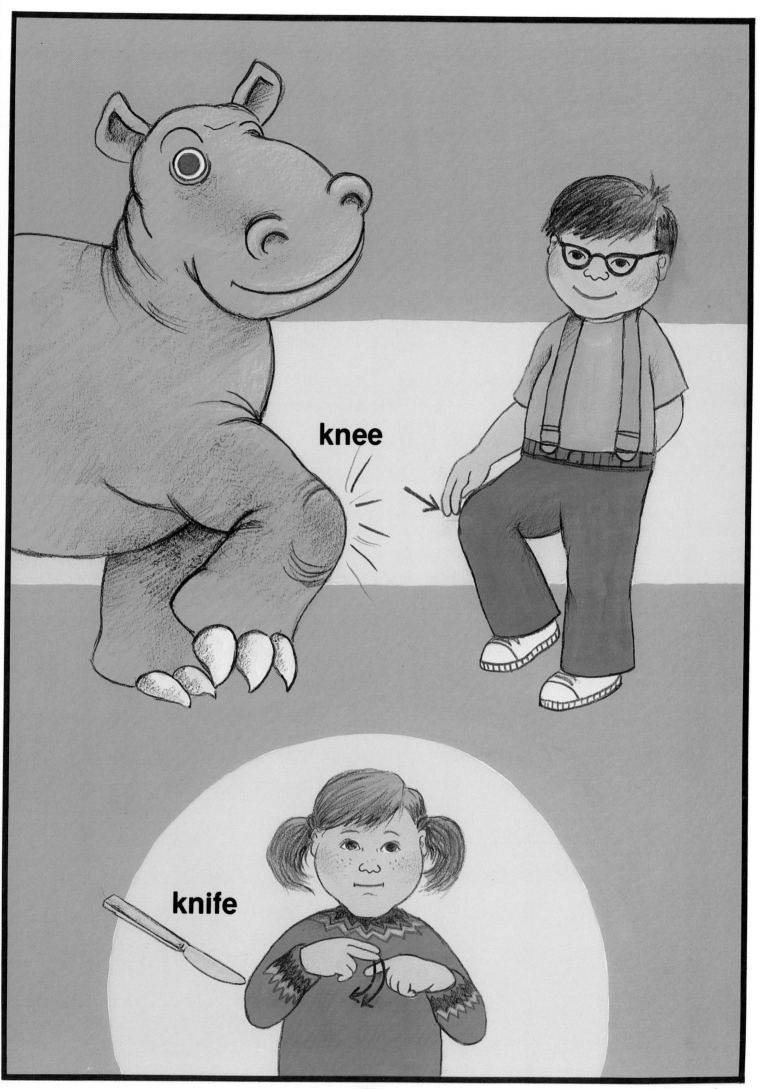

knee

knife

Ll

ladder

lamb

leaf

leg

letter

DEAR MOM,
I MISS
YOU VERY
MUCH. TAKE
CARE OF MY
FISH.
LOVE
BILLY

light

lion

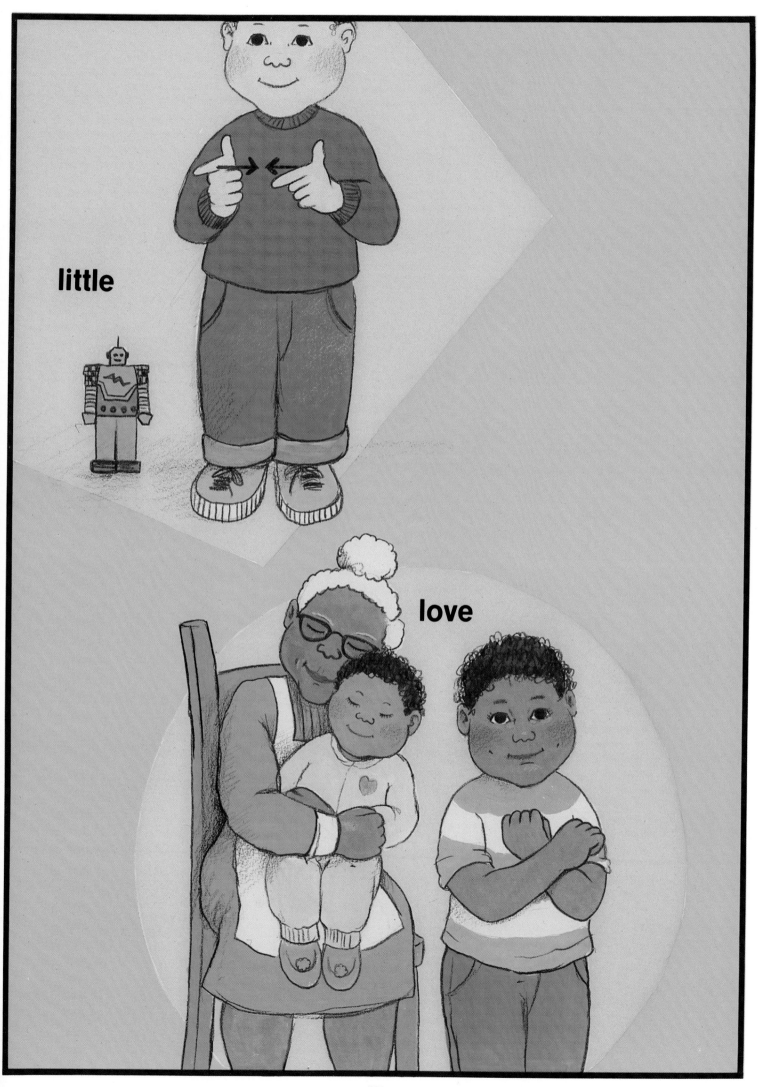

little

love

Mm

man

meat

milk

moon

mouse

mouth

Oo

open

orange

owl

Pp

paint

pants

pencil

picture

pig

Qq

queen

Rr

rabbit

rain

read

ring

44

room

run

45

Ss

school

ship

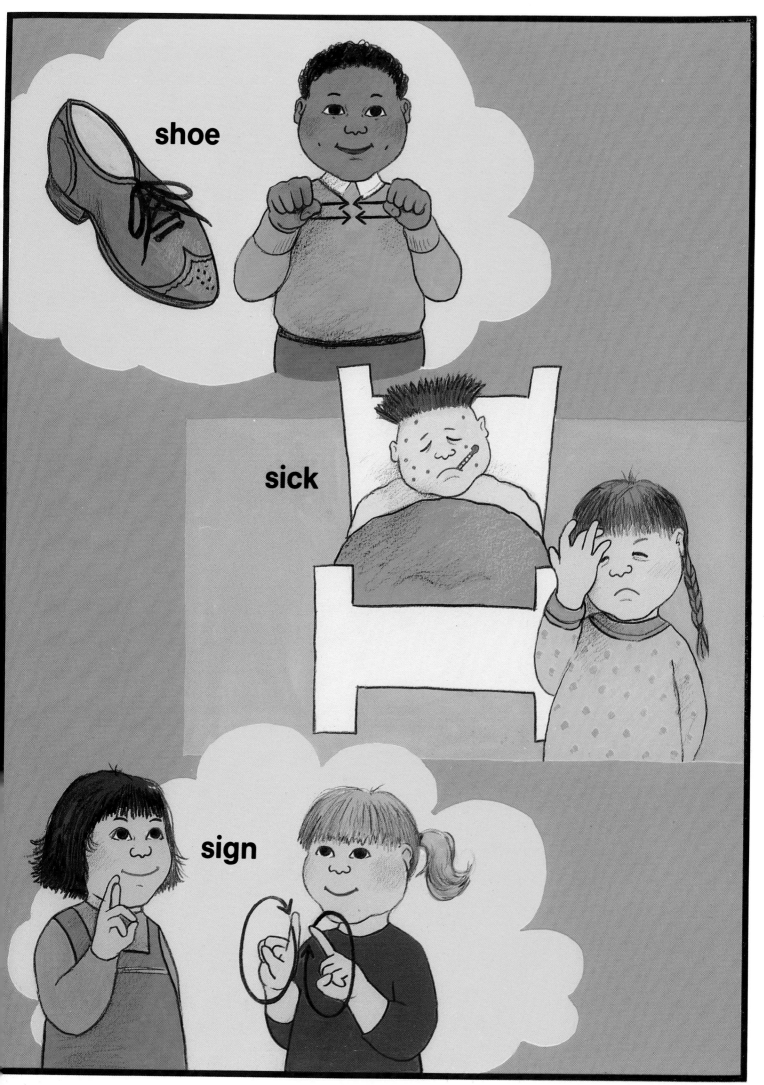

shoe

sick

sign

47

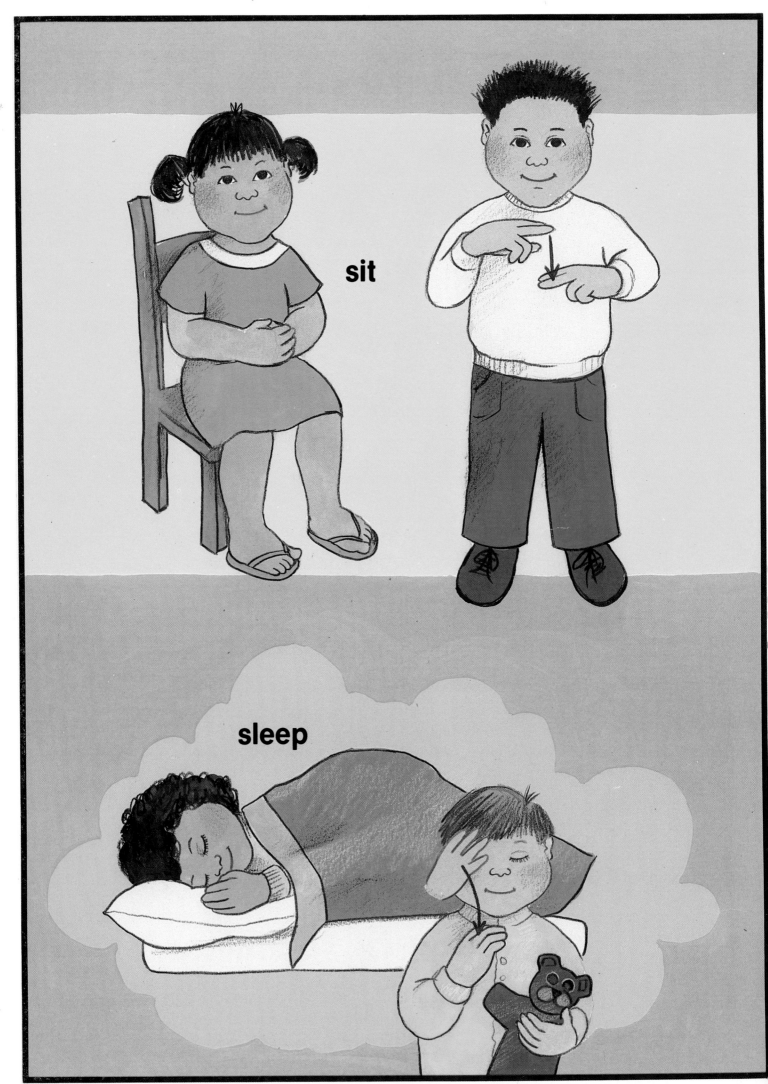

sit

sleep

48

snow

sock

soft

49

spoon

stand

star

sun

swim

Tt

table

talk

telephone

52

television

toilet

tongue

train

tree

Uu

umbrella

under

Vv

valentine

visit

Ww

walk

wash

water

window

woman

58

Xx

xylophone

Yy

young

yo-yo

Zz

zebra

zipper

A Letter to Parents

We began signing with our daughter when she was fifteen months old, shortly after finding out that she was severe to profoundly hearing impaired. Prior to receiving this news, we had been wondering why this beautiful, alert baby of ours wouldn't pay attention to anything we said. In fact, it was the frustration of not being able to "get through," of not being able to communicate life's daily events, that at last made us admit to ourselves that she wasn't hearing us and made us take her for a hearing test.

When we first began to sign, we felt like we were "all thumbs," and we felt overwhelmed by the task of learning "all those signs." Within weeks, our nervousness eased when it was obvious that our daughter understood what we signed. Nervousness was replaced by excitement when, shortly after that, she began to sign to us.

As our nervousness lessened, sign language began to feel like a natural extension of the gestures we had always used in talking with anyone. The signs we needed or wanted for talking with a baby were often mimes or so literally representational that they were easy to remember. There was no need to be fluent before starting to sign to our baby. As soon as we had learned a sign, we ran for a picture or the object itself, or began drawing a picture or acting out the action so we could teach the sign to our daughter. This was just the same as parents teaching their hearing children their first words by pointing at things and naming them verbally. We had been doing this, without success, since our daughter was born. Now with sign she was learning language as fast as we could show it to her. She showed such delight in learning that she spurred us on to learn more.

As we learned more sign language we put together sentences. We signed in English word order because that was what was most comfortable for us. As with a hearing baby's first words, the first signs our daughter made were single signs, next two signs put together, then phrases, and finally sentences. But unlike a hearing child, she had a way of expressing whole sentences worth of information before she could even put two signs together. Seeing a beach ball, she signed *ball* but with her hands spread wide, showing us she noticed it was a *big* ball. On visiting an airport, she signed *airplane,* then made the sign swoop and land, showing us that she had noticed far more than just the existence of the airplane.

Suddenly we had a way of saying, "Don't hit the boy," or "Come eat", or "Need the toilet?" or "Good girl. We love you." If a deaf adult had wanted to sign to us about more than cats and milk, we would have been stuck—but we were communicating with our baby and that was the important thing. Our daughter's behavior and mood improved too. We had known *we* were frustrated, but we had not really realized how frustrated *she* was until suddenly she had a way of expressing her choices. She could sign *juice,* instead of screaming and shoving the milk off the high chair tray if we made the wrong choice for her. She could sign *out,* if she wanted to go outside, instead of standing by the door and weeping. Without sign language, we would have missed the beauty of her early thoughts. Without sign language, she would not have developed the self-esteem that hearing children are developing at this toddler and preschool age by communicating and manipulating their surroundings. And as we watched her develop into a lovely little individual, we were able to relax and put her hearing impairment in its true perspective. We went from feeling like "we have a DEAF daughter" (letting the impairment be her identity) to feeling like "we have a wonderful child who has blue eyes, blonde hair, and not very much hearing" (realizing that her deafness was just one of the many things that made her herself).

With her frustration minimized by being able to communicate in a language that was clear, our daughter had energy for the other skills she was tackling at the same time. Some of these were skills that all preschoolers must develop, for example, sharing or potty training. Other skills were those related to her hearing impairment, such as auditory training and speech training.

Sign language was indispensable in auditory training, which we began as soon as she received her first hearing aid at age sixteen months. We could sign, "I hear the telephone," while we put her hand on the ringing phone, and know that she knew what we were saying. That way she could concentrate on listening for the sound, rather than having to use half her concentration trying to figure out what we'd said. As she learned to use her residual hearing so she could sort out one sound from a background of fuzz, and as she learned that sound was something useful and something to respond to, she had a way of telling us "telephone!" when she'd heard it.

She had always watched our lips move and had sometimes imitated that. But, when she had a language base to help her sort out what those flapping lips meant and a language base to give her something she wanted to say, she began to speak. It was no more clear at first than any child's baby talk, but we had the advantage of being able to clarify with signs: "Did you say ball or dog?" We could also use fingerspelling to emphasize the sounds and lip movements she missed: "Ball had *L*." Her articulation improved rapidly.

Sign is still very helpful in teaching her new vocabulary. And sign language will be vital for her participation in the deaf culture as she grows older. However, now that she is seven years old and comfortably bilingual, we have a choice when we communicate. We can have a spoken conversation if the room is quiet but, at other times, signing is much handier. Besides, it's fun! I can "yell" to her across the yard by signing larger (she'd never be able to speechread or hear my voice from that distance). We can share secrets (signing very small). We can communicate when her hearing aids are off (in the bathtub, at the lake, or in bed at night).

Each of the 150 words in this book, chosen from various published lists of children's early vocabularies, is presented in the three forms: a picture, a drawing of the sign, and the object pictured. If you and your child are learning sign simultaneously, you should be able to read the book together without having to look up signs or pictures in other books (during which time you've lost the baby's attention). The signers are all children so your child can see that children sign.

No part of this process occurred for us without the help and constant reassurances of many wonderful and loving people. If you are deaf parents, I thank you for your generosity in sharing your language with us. Perhaps the only way to begin to thank those who have gone before us is to give something to those who come after us. It is in this spirit that I offer this book.

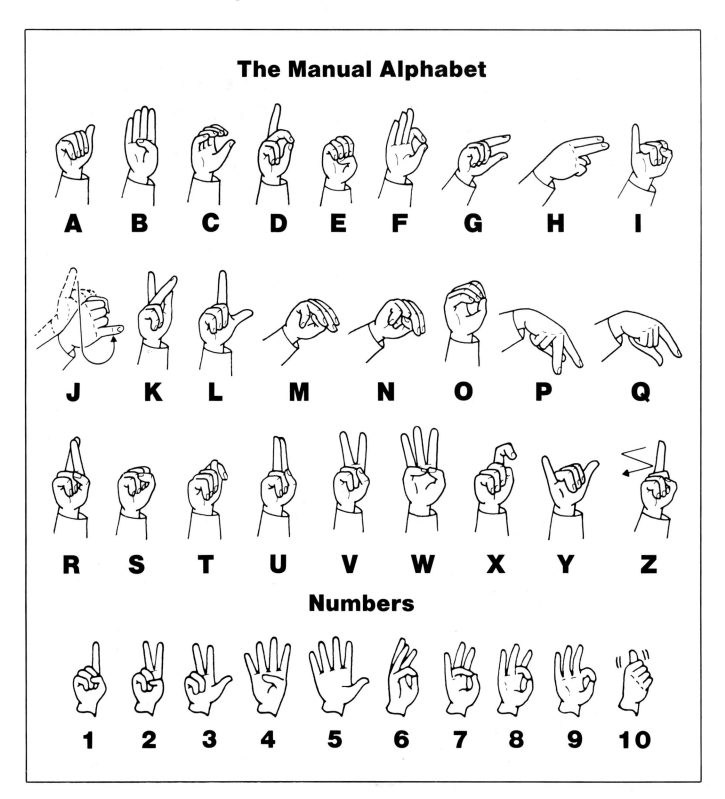

The Manual Alphabet

A B C D E F G H I
J K L M N O P Q
R S T U V W X Y Z

Numbers

1 2 3 4 5 6 7 8 9 10

How to Use This Book

Fingerspelling

The manual alphabet (fingerspelled alphabet) is shown on page 62. Any word for which there is no sign or for which you don't remember the sign can be fingerspelled. Also, many of the fingerspelled letters are used as handshapes in making signs.

Fingerspelling is done with whichever hand you normally use as a right-handed or left-handed person. Your palm faces out (that is, away from your body) except for the letters *g* and *h* where your palm and extended fingers point toward the center. Hold your hand in front of your chest or in front of the area between your shoulder and mouth. The position of your hand should be what is most comfortable for you but close enough to your mouth so that your mouth and hand are visible together. Say the word, not the individual letters, as you fingerspell. Your fingers move but your hand does not. The exception is in words that contain double letters. For most, form the first of the double letters. Then while holding the shape of the letter, move your hand from the center slightly to the side with a small bounce. In words with double letters made with a closed hand-shape (for example, *o*, *s*, and *t)*, open your hand slightly between the two letters.

Signing

Right-handed versus left-handed signers

The illustrations in this book show all right-handed signers, and the directions refer to the right hand and the left hand. However, if you are left-handed, reverse the hand designations in the illustrations and descriptions.

Three aspects of signs

There are three aspects to each sign: the shape of the hand or hands, the position of the hands, and the movement as the hands go from one shape and position to another shape and/or position.

1. **Handshape(s)**

    The handshapes refer to the shapes of the hand used for letters of the alphabet and numbers (see p. 62) and modified handshapes (below). When a sign is made with only one hand, that hand is the one you normally use as a right-handed or a left-handed person. The other hand is held at waist level or to the side.

2. **Position**

    In the written descriptions, position refers to the orientation of the palms and fingers and the location of the hands at the beginning of the sign. The ending position is described along with the movement. In the illustrations, the beginning positions of the hands are outlined in red, the ending positions are outlined in black. The signs are done in front of the chest, unless otherwise indicated. The orientation of the hand is the same as for fingerspelling (palm out, fingers up) unless otherwise indicated.

3. **Movement**

    The written descriptions tell how the hands and body move in forming the sign and also how many times the movement is repeated. In the illustrations, movement is shown by an arrow for a single movement, double arrows for a repeated movement, and two-headed arrows for back and forth movements.

Modified Handshapes

open hand

fingers together; thumb slightly out

claw shape hand

fingers and thumb pulled back and curled

flat O hand

thumb tip meeting fingertips, fingers as straight as possible while still meeting thumb

bent V hand

first two fingers (V), curled toward palm

bent B hand

fingers together and bent forward at right angle to hand; thumb tight against hand and at right angle to fingers

Illustrations reproduced from *The Comprehensive Signed English Dictionary* by permission of Gallaudet University Press, 800 Florida Avenue NE, Washington, D.C.

Sign Descriptions

Aa

airplane

handshape:	thumb, index finger, and little finger are extended, middle fingers tucked under
position:	hand just above shoulder, palm down, tips forward
movement:	hand moves a short distance forward once

apple

handshape:	bent index finger
position:	palm down; knuckle of bent finger touches cheek
movement:	twist hand until palm is toward tody

arm

handshapes:	right hand C, left hand open
position:	left hand palm down, C hand clasps wrist of open hand, thumb below, fingers above
movement:	C hand moves up from wrist to elbow

Bb

baby

handshapes:	both hands open
position:	right arm lying in left arm at waist height, both palms up, fingertips to sides
movement:	arms rock as if rocking a baby

ball

handshapes:	claw hands
position:	hands slightly apart, palms facing, thumbs below
movement:	bring hands together so fingertips touch

bear

handshapes:	claw hands
position:	arms crossed over chest, palms toward body, fingers up
movement:	scratch upper chest twice

bed

handshape:	open
position:	palm against cheek, fingertips up
movement:	tilt head slightly

big

handshapes:	both hands B
position:	hands slightly apart, palms facing, fingertips out
movement:	move hands further apart

bird

handshape:	G
position:	place back of hand on chin
movement:	touch index finger to thumb twice

birthday

This is a two part sign—**birth** followed smoothly by **day**.

birth

handshapes:	both hands open
position:	place palm of right hand across chest, left arm in front of waist, palm up
movement:	bring right hand down into left hand, both palms up

day

handshapes:	right hand D, left hand open
position:	left arm across body at waist height, palm down, fingertips to side; D points up, palm toward center; elbow of right arm sits on the back of left hand
movement:	right arm folds down until right hand D is on elbow of left arm

blow

handshapes:	right hand O, left hand D
position:	O right hand palm down, fingertips out, back of hand near mouth; D out in front of chin, palm to side, tip up, mimicking a candle
movement:	O hand opens up into 5 as it moves toward D

boat

handshapes:	both hands slightly cupped
position:	both palms up, fingertips out, hands together along little finger edges, forming a boat shape
movement:	move hands forward twice with a slight bouncing motion

book

handshapes:	both hands open
position:	palms together, thumbs up
movement	open the hands, ending with palms up and little finger edges of hands together, as a book being opened

box

handshapes:	both hands open
position:	hands apart, palms facing, thumbs up, forming sides of box
movement:	turn hands so palms are toward body, right hand away from body and left hand close to body, forming front and back of box

boy

handshape:	flat O
position:	palm down, fingertips to side, hand at head with fingertips at midforehead
movement:	open and close O as if touching the brim of a boy's cap

broken

handshapes:	both hands S
position:	hands together along thumbs and index finger sides, palms down
movement:	turn hands, ending with palms facing and hands apart

Note: This is also the sign for **break.**

brush

handshape:	A
position:	hand at side of head with palm side on hair, little finger edge of hand forward
movement:	brush downward twice

button

handshape:	index finger curled inside of thumb to form a small circle, other fingers extended
position:	place circle near top of chest, palm to side
movement:	tap chest three times while moving circle downward

Cc
cake

handshapes:	right hand claw shape, left hand open
position:	left hand palm up, fingertips out; fingertips of claw hand in palm of open hand, like cake on a plate
movement:	lift claw hand

candle

handshapes:	right hand 5, left hand D
position:	5 hand palm out, fingertips up; D hand palm in, fingertip up; fingertip of D hand on palm side of wrist of 5 hand
movement:	wiggle fingers of 5 hand like flickering candle flame

car

handshapes:	both hands C
position:	hands apart with palms toward body, one hand high, one hand low
movement:	alternate hands in semicircular motion like turning a steering wheel

Note: The initialized version of this sign would use A hands for automobile, B hands for bus, and T hands for truck.

cat

handshape:	9
position:	thumb and index finger of 9 hand at side of mouth, palm toward center
movement:	pull hand sideways twice, indicating whiskers

catch

handshapes:	claw hands
position:	left palm sideways, thumb toward body; right hand is further from body with palm out and thumb toward side
movement:	bring right hand backwards while forming a fist, ending with fist in the other palm

chair

handshapes:	right hand N, left hand C
position:	C hand palm toward center, thumb down; N hand palm out; first two fingers of N hand hang over thumb of C hand
movement:	none

climb

handshape: bent V

position: palm out, fingers up

movement: hand moves up while making small semicircles with open part of semicircles toward center line

clock

handshapes: right hand one, left hand A

position: A hand palm down

movement: tap back of A hand wrist with fingertip of right hand one; then bring hands up to outline a clock by making C shapes with both hands facing each other

coat

handshapes: both hands A

position: palms down, thumbs touching chest near tips of collar

movement: move hands down in semicircles, as if tracing lapels of coat with thumbs

comb

handshape: claw hand

position: fingers up, fingertips and palm to side of hair

movement: move hand down through hair twice

come

handshapes: both hands one

position: palms up, fingertips forward

movement: bend arms more at elbows bringing hands up and toward chest (movement in opposite direction from **go**)

cookie

handshapes: right hand claw, left hand open

position: left hand palm up, fingertips out; fingertips of claw hand in palm of open hand

movement: twist claw hand as if cutting out cookies

cow

handshape: Y

position: thumb of Y hand to temple, palm forward, little finger up high, like a cow's horn

movement: twist hand forward until palm is down and knuckles face the center

cry

handshapes: both hands one

position: index fingertips under eyes, palms toward cheeks

movement: draw fingertips downward twice as if tracing tears

cup

handshapes: right hand X, left hand open

position: left hand palm up, thumb out; X hand palm in, hooked finger toward center; little finger side of X hand sits in palm of open hand like a cup in a saucer

movement: none

Dd
dirty

handshape: 5

position: back of hand under chin, fingertips to side

movement: wiggle fingers

dog

handshape: open

position: palm against thigh

movement: pat thigh twice

doll

handshape: X

position: palm sideways, hook of X on bridge of nose

movement: brush down to tip of nose twice

door

handshapes: both hands B

position: hands together along index fingers, palms facing out but a little down

movement: turn right hand so palm is up and towards body, then return to starting position

draw

handshapes: right hand I, left hand open

position: fingertips of open hand up, palm toward center; I hand palm in, tip up and touching open hand palm near top

movement: draw I finger down palm in wavy motion

dress

handshapes: both hands 5

position: hands apart and at top of chest, palms in, fingertips towards center

movement: brush hands down chest while moving hands slightly further apart; repeat

drink

handshape: C

position: C in front of chin, palm facing center, thumb toward body, fingers forward

movement: tip C up to lips as if drinking, ending with thumb at lips, fingers up

drive

handshapes: both hands A

position: palms in, one hand high, one hand low

movement: move high hand down and low hand up in semicircles; repeat

Note: This sign is sometimes initialized by using D hands.

dry

handshape: X

position: X hand palm down, fingers sideways, hook against chin

movement: pull X across chin

duck

handshape: thumb touching tips of index and middle fingers

position: back of hand to chin

movement: snap thumb and fingers together twice like duck quacking

Ee

ear

handshape: G

position: earlobe held between thumb and finger

movement: none

eat

handshape: flat O

position: hand slight distance from mouth, fingertips pointed toward lips

movement: move hand to lips and away several times

egg

handshapes: both hands H

position: palms toward body

movement: bring fingers of right hand H down across fingers of left hand H, then draw hands apart and down as if cracking an egg

elephant

handshape: fingers together and curved forward

position: back of hand to nose

movement: move hand forward and down tracing elephant's trunk

eye

handshape: one

position: palm in, finger up and touching eye

movement: none

Ff

face

handshape: one

position: palm in, finger to center and pointing to near side of chin

movement: draw circle up and around face

fall

handshapes: right hand V, left hand open

position: left hand palm up, tips out; V hand palm in, tips standing in open hand palm

movement: flip V forward and over, ending with V palm up

fence

handshapes: both hands 4

position: palms in, fingertips toward center with tips of middle fingers touching

movement: move hands apart

finger

handshapes: both hands one

position: palms down

movement: tap index finger of right hand on left index finger

fire

handshapes: both hands 5 with slightly curled fingers

position: hands apart, palms toward body, fingertips up

movement: flutter fingers while moving hands up, indicating flickering flames

fish

handshapes: both hands open

position: palm of right hand facing center, tips forward; left hand palm in, tips touching inside of wrist of right hand

movement: flutter right hand while moving both hands forward

floor

handshapes: both hands B

position: palms down, fingertips forward, sides of index fingers touching

movement: move hands apart

flower

handshape: flat O

position: palm toward face, tips on right side of the nose

movement: move fingers in an arc to other side of nose

fork

handshapes: right hand V, left hand open

position: left hand palm up, tips toward center, V tips down

movement: tap open palm with tips of V

frog

handshape: S

position: back of S hand under chin, knuckles toward side

movement: flick index and middle fingers out to V twice

Gg
girl

handshape: A

position: palm toward cheek, thumb touching top of cheek

movement: move thumb in arc down jawline as if indicating tie of bonnet

glass

handshapes: right hand C, left hand open

position: left hand palm up, tips toward center; little finger side of C sits in open palm

movement: raise C up as if outlining a tall glass

go

handshapes: both hands one

position: hands apart, palms out, fingertips up

movement: move hands down, ending with palms down (movement in opposite direction from **come**)

grow

handshapes: right hand flat O, left hand C

position: C hand thumb in, fingers out; flat O hand palm in, fingertips up

movement: move fingertips of flat O up through C, spreading O fingers as hand emerges above C, like a plant growing

Hh
hair

handshape: F

position: hold hair at side of head with thumb and index finger

movement: none

hand

handshapes: both hands open

position: left hand fingertips out and palm slanted toward center

movement: draw little finger side of right hand across side of wrist of left hand

happy

handshape: open

position: palm on chest, fingertips toward center

movement: brush up chest twice in quick, short motions

hat

handshape: open

position: palm down, fingertips toward center

movement: tap top of head

head

handshape:	bent B
position:	fingertips to temple
movement:	move fingertips down and touch side of chin without touching cheek in between

hearing aid

handshape:	thumb touching tips of index and middle fingers
position:	palm down, fingertips on center of ear, as if inserting aid
movement:	none

hit

handshapes:	right hand S; left hand one
position:	left hand one with tip up and palm toward center
movement:	first strikes index finger

horse

handshape:	H with thumb extended
position:	thumb to temple, H fingers up and forward
movement:	flap H fingers downward twice

hot

handshape:	claw hand
position:	fingertips on mouth
movement:	twist hand away from mouth quickly, ending with palm down

house

handshapes:	both hands open
position:	tips of both hands meet to form roof
movement:	move hands apart then down to finish roof and form sides of house

Ii

ice cream

handshape:	S
position:	index finger side of hand at mouth
movement:	move hand down twice, as if licking an ice cream cone

iron

handshapes:	right hand A, left hand open
position:	left hand palm up, fingertips toward center; A hand knuckles down, palm toward body; A knuckles sit on open palm
movement:	move A back and forth from palm to fingertips of open hand as if ironing

Jj

jam

handshapes:	right hand I, left hand open
position:	left hand palm up, fingertips out; I hand palm down, tip of I in open palm
movement:	flick I across open palm and up, drawing a J; then change right hand to M and circle M on open palm as if spreading jam

juice

handshape:	I
position:	tip up, palm out
movement:	fingerspell letter J; then change handshape to C with palm sideways and thumb at mouth; tip C up; literally J plus **drink**

jump

handshapes:	right hand V, left hand open
position:	left hand palm up, fingertips out; tips of V in open palm
movement:	pull V up quickly while changing shape to bent V; repeat

Kk

key

handshapes:	right hand X; left hand open
position:	left hand palm facing center, fingertips out; knuckle of X index finger in open palm
movement:	twist X back and forth in open palm

kiss

handshape:	open
position:	palm in, fingertips up and at mouth
movement:	move fingertips to cheek without turning hand

knee

handshape: bent B

position: arm extended downward, palm toward leg

movement: raise knee and touch with fingertips

knife

handshapes: right hand H; left hand one

position: left hand palm down, fingertip toward center

movement: strike tips of H against one and move outward; repeat

Ll

ladder

handshapes: right hand bent V; left hand one

position: left hand palm out, fingertip up

movement: walk index and middle fingers of bent V up back of one index finger

lamb

handshapes: right hand L, left hand open

position: open hand palm up, arm across body; L hand palm up, resting on wrist of open hand

movement: move L hand up left arm toward elbow, as if clipping wool; repeat

leaf

handshapes: right hand 5; left hand one

position: 5 hand fingertips hang down, palm toward body; left hand palm in, fingertip to side and touching inside of 5 hand wrist

movement: pivot 5 from side to side on tip of one

leg

handshape: open hand

position: arm extended downwards

movement: pat thigh with open palm

letter

handshapes: right hand A; left hand open

position: left hand palm up, fingertips out; A hand palm in, thumb on mouth

movement: bring thumb of A down to open palm, as if putting a stamp on a letter

light

handshape: flat O

position: O palm down, fingertips out, hand beside head

movement: drop O fingers down into 5 shape, palm down

lion

handshape: claw hand

position: claw palm down, fingertips forward; hand on top of head, fingertips at forehead

movement: move hand straight back to back of head, indicating lion's mane

little

handshapes: both hands L

position: hands apart, palms facing, fingertips out, thumbs up

movement: bring hands close together

love

handshapes: both hands S

position: arms crossed at wrists, left hand to inside

movement: place crossed wrists over heart (that is, on the chest slightly to the left of center)

Mm

man

handshape: open hand

position: palm sideways, fingertips up, thumb touching midforehead

movement: arc hand downward until thumb touches chest

meat

handshapes: right hand F, left hand open

position: left hand palm in, fingertips toward center; hold flesh between thumb and index finger of open hand with thumb and index finger of F hand

movement: wiggle F hand

milk

handshapes: claw hands

position: palms in, thumbs up

movement: move hands up and down alternately while squeezing them into S shapes; repeat, as if milking a cow

moon

handshape: thumb and index finger curved to form a crescent

position: hand beside eye, palm and open part of crescent toward center

movement: none

mouse

handshape: one

position: palm toward center, fingertip up, fingertip beside nose

movement: bending at wrist, move hand down and to side, flicking tip of nose with fingertip; repeat

mouth

handshape: one

position: palm in, tip up and by corner of mouth

movement: draw a small horizontal oval in front of mouth with fingertip

Nn
neck

handshape: bent B

position: palm and fingertips toward center

movement: tap side of neck with fingertips twice

nose

handshape: one

position: palm toward center, fingertip up and touching side of nose

movement: none

Oo
open

handshapes: both hands B

position: palms down, fingertips out, index fingers touching

movement: arc hands apart, ending with palms up

orange

handshape: C

position: hand at mouth, palm toward center

movement: squeeze hand into S shape; repeat as if squeezing an orange

owl

handshapes: both hands O

position: O hands in front of eyes

movement: twist hands toward center slightly while looking through O's; repeat

Pp
paint

handshapes: right hand B, left hand open

position: left hand palm toward center, fingertips up; B hand palm down, tips toward center

movement: flap fingertips of B hand up and down open hand palm, as if brushing paint on palm

pants

handshapes: both hands open

position: palms on fronts of hips

movement: brush fingertips up to waist while bending hands into bent B's

pencil

handshapes: right hand index fingertip touching tip of thumb, left hand open

position: left hand palm up, fingertips out and toward center; right hand palm in, tips to mouth

movement: move right hand down and slide tips along open hand palm from heel of hand to fingertips

picture

handshapes: right hand C; left hand open

position: index finger and thumb side of C hand on temple; left hand fingertips up, palm toward center

movement: bring side of C down into open palm

pig

handshape: open hand

position: palm down, back of hand under chin

movement: flap fingers down into bent B

Qq

queen

handshape: Q

position: palm down, thumb on opposite shoulder

movement: bring hand diagonally down and across chest to waist

Rr

rabbit

handshapes: both hands U

position: arms crossed at wrists, right hand to outside, so backs of hands face each other and fingertips are mostly up

movement: wiggle U fingers down and up

rain

handshapes: claw hands

position: hands apart, palms down, fingertips out

movement: move hands down two or three times

read

handshapes: right hand V, left hand open

position: left hand palm toward center, fingertips up; V hand palm down, fingertips pointing toward fingertips of open palm

movement: move tips of V back and forth as they move down open palm

ring

handshapes: right hand F; left hand 5

position: 5 hand palm down, fingertips toward center; F hand palm down, fingertips out

movement: move the circle formed by the F hand up the ring finger as if sliding on a ring

room

handshapes: both hands R

position: hands apart, palms facing, fingertips out

movement: turn hands so palms are toward body, with left hand closer to body

Note: This is the same as the sign for **box** but uses R hands instead of B hands.

run

handshapes: both hands L

position: index fingertips out, thumbs up; right hand index finger hooked around thumb of left hand

movement: wiggle L fingers and thumbs while moving both hands forward

Ss

school

handshapes: both hands open

position: left hand palm up, fingertips out; right hand above left hand, palm down, tips to side

movement: clap top hand onto bottom hand twice

ship

handshapes: right hand 3, left hand open

position: left hand palm up, fingertips out; 3 hand palm toward center, fingertips out; little finger side of 3 hand lying in open palm

movement: move 3 forward toward fingertips of open hand twice

shoe

handshapes: both hands S

position: hands apart, palms down, knuckles out

movement: strike index finger sides of hands together twice

sick

handshape: 5

position: palm toward face, fingertips up

movement: tap forehead with tip of middle finger once

sign (as in sign language)

handshapes: both hands one

position: hands apart, palms out, fingertips up, one hand slightly higher than other

movement: circle index fingers in toward body alternately (that is, so that one hand is up while the other is down and one hand is forward while the other is back)

sit

handshapes: both hands H

position: palms down, fingertips toward center, H fingers of right hand slightly above those of left hand

movement: bring right hand H fingers down to rest on left hand H fingers

sleep

handshape: 5

position: palm toward face, fingertips up and at forehead

movement: draw hand down over face while closing fingers, ending in flat O shape in front of chin

snow

handshapes: both hands 5

position: hands apart, palms down, fingertips out

movement: move hands down slowly while wiggling fingers

socks

handshapes: both hands S with extended index fingers

position: palms down, index fingers pointing down, hands touching along index finger sides of hands

movement: rub one hand forward and the other back, then reverse; repeat movement several times

soft

handshapes: claw hands

position: hands apart, palms up, fingertips forward

movement: more hands down slightly while closing fingers into flat O shapes, palms up; repeat

spoon

handshapes: right hand H, left hand open

position: both hands palm up, fingertips toward center; fingers of H hand lying lengthwise in open palm

movement: raise H fingers to mouth, as if eating from a spoon; repeat

stand

handshapes: right hand V; left hand open

position: left hand palm up, fingertips toward center; V hand palm in, fingertips down and standing in open palm

movement: none

star

handshapes: both hands one

position: palms out, fingertips up, hands touching along index fingers

movement: strike index fingers upward against each other alternately

sun

handshape: C

position: tips of C against side of eye

movement: none

swim

handshapes: both hands cupped

position: palms down, fingertips out, hands together along index fingers

movement: move hands forward and away from each other, repeat as if doing breast stroke

Tt

table

handshapes: both hands B

position: palms down, fingertips out, hands together along index fingers

movement: move hands apart; then turn hands so palms are facing and thumbs are up; move hands downward slightly, as if outlining top, then sides of a table

talk

handshapes: both hands one

position: palms facing, right index finger pointed at mouth, left index finger pointed out and up

movement: twist hands at wrists, moving right finger away from mouth and left finger toward mouth; repeat

telephone

handshape: Y

position: thumb on ear, little finger just below mouth

movement: none

television

handshape:	T
position:	palm out, thumb tip up
movement:	change T to V, fingerspelling **TV** in single movement

toilet

handshape:	T
position:	palm out, thumb tip up
movement:	shake hand in short movements from side to side several times

tongue

handshape:	one
position:	tongue sticking out slightly; point to tip of tongue
movement:	none

train

handshapes:	both hands H
position:	palms down, fingertips toward center; right hand H fingers crosswise on top of left hand H fingers
movement:	move right hand H fingers back and forth from knuckles to fingertips of left hand H

tree

handshapes:	right hand 5, left hand open
position:	left hand palm down, fingertips to side, arm across waist; 5 hand palm facing center, fingertips up; elbow of right arm resting on back of left hand, like a tree trunk meeting the ground
movement:	twist right hand back and forth rapidly, indicating moving treetop

Uu
umbrella

handshapes:	both hands S
position:	palms toward body, index finger sides of hands up; right hand S sits on top of left hand S
movement:	move right hand up, as if opening an umbrella

under

handshapes:	right hand A with thumb extended, left hand open
position:	left hand palm down, fingertips toward center; A hand palm toward center, thumb up; open hand forward of A hand
movement:	pass A hand under open palm

Vv
valentine

handshapes:	both hands V
position:	palms in, fingertips toward center and slightly down; fingertips touching left chest
movement:	outline a heart shape on chest

visit

handshapes:	both hands V
position:	palms in, fingertips up, one hand a little further out from body than other
movement:	rotate hands away from body alternately

Ww
walk

handshapes:	both hands open
position:	palms down, fingertips out
movement:	flap hands down alternately several times while moving hands forward

wash

handshapes:	right hand S, left hand open
position:	left hand palm up, fingertips toward center; S hand in open palm
movement:	rub S in circular motion in palm

water

handshape:	W
position:	palm to center, fingertips up
movement:	tap corner of lips (or center of chin) twice with index finger of W

window

handshapes:	both hands open
position:	palms in, fingertips to sides, right hand little finger on index finger of left hand
movement:	move top hand up, then down, as if opening and closing a window

woman

handshape: A with thumb extended

position: tip of thumb at top of cheek

movement: bring thumb down jawline; then bring hand toward chest while changing into open hand, palm to side, fingertips up; touch thumb to chest

Note: This is the sign **girl** followed by the sign **fine**.

Xx
xylophone

handshapes: both hands A

position: hands apart, palms facing, thumbs on top

movement: move hands up and down alternately, as if playing a xylophone

Yy
young

handshapes: both hands bent B

position: hands apart, palms toward body, thumbs up; fingertips on upper chest

movement: brush fingers up chest twice

yo-yo

handshape: A

position: hand near shoulder, palm forward, thumb toward center

movement: drop hand down while opening into a 5 shape, palm and fingertips slanted down; repeat

Zz
zebra

handshapes: both hands 4

position: palms in, fingertips toward center; fingertips near top center of chest

movement: move hands apart as if drawing stripes across chest with fingertips; move hands down and repeat

zipper

handshape: A

position: hand on lower chest, palm toward body, thumb on top

movement: move hand up and down chest as if opening and closing a zipper

Index